The Gift of Light

Elizabeth Burns

diehard
Edinburgh

diehard publishers
3 Spittal Street
Edinburgh
EH3 9DY

ISBN 0 946230 63 3
© Elizabeth Burns 1999

British Library Cataloguing in Publication Data
A catalog record for this book is
available from the British Library

The Publisher acknowledges the financial assistance of the
Scottish Arts Council in the publication of this volume.

The Publisher acknowledges an award from the Deric Bolton
Poetry Trust towards the publication of this volume.

Several of these poems have previously appeared in
*Asheville Poetry Review, Cambridge Journal of
Comparative Literature, Carapace, Chapman, Edinburgh
Review, Fifelines, Kronos, Lines Review, New Orleans
Review, Nomad, Northlight, Poetry Scotland, Scottish
Child, Second Shift, Tablines, Pomegranate* (Stramullion)
and *The Golden Goose Hour* (Taranis Books).

Other **diehard** poetry

Light Caught Bending, Martha Modena Vertreace
Second Mourning, Martha Modena Vertreace
Millennial, Sally Evans
The Divine Joker, Richard Livermore
Thirteen Ways of Looking at The Highlands, Colin Will
Saving Graces, Stuart A. Paterson
Waiting in Waikato, Angus Calder
Life, Bashabi Fraser
Deepwater Terminal, Morelle Smith
Perfume & petrol fumes, Richard Price
Aultgrishan, Ian Blake

poetry related

Gang Doun wi a Sang: play (about William Soutar), Joy Hendry
Walking Through Apocalypse, Alan Jackson

diehard also publishes
the broadsheet quarterly *Poetry Scotland*.

CONTENTS

I Dragons

II Memorials

III The Gift of Light

I
Dragons

Dragons in the carpark

Break up the tarmac
of a carpark in Quebec
and you'll find Chinatown

You'll find the carcass
of an old laundry
the skull of the laundryman
still bound with a blue rag

You'll find his iron, rusted
and a birdcage with a scrap
of songbird left inside
You'll find an ink-brush, hardened
disintegrating paper
and a sliver of calligraphy
You'll find shards of molten glass
and mah-jong tiles of ivory

Dig, and you'll forget the rotten, fetid stink
remember instead fresh fish and lemon juice
the perfume of roses, smoky tea

Dig, and you'll find the teeth of old men
fallen from soft gums, a pool of wax-melt
unstrung beads, umbrella spikes
crumbled leather shoes
and a shabby suitcase lying open like a mouth

Dig, and you'll find the scales of dragons
Dig, and you'll remember festivals of fire —
how you danced and sang then
when dragons pranced the streets
swishing their green and scarlet tails
and flying, it seemed, with gorgeous wings

And how you'd set your paper lanterns on the river
dreamed they'd sail as far as ice floes
but saw the candles falter and the lanterns drown
beneath the weight of sodden paper

Dig, and you'll let the dragons out again
out into the trampled carpark
See them take the tin cars in their mouths
spit them onto bulldozed land

See, as your fingers trawl for memories
for scraps of bone and gold
see, as the sidewalk cracks apart
the dragons of your childhood
rising, breathing fire —

At Barra airport

We've wandered all morning on the runway,
dabbling in seawater for shells,
looking out to Eriskay
and the blue Uists.

Reaching the airport, we go in for coffee,
windswept, sand on our shoes.
The phone rings but no one answers it.
All the chairs are turned towards the view.

Out again, with the ocean
humming in our ears,
we sit down to picnic on the dunes
and up snuggles the airport cat.

People begin to gather: porters,
the post bus, an ambulance,
a man with cameras.
Everyone eyes the horizon.

And here it comes now, out of the clouds,
dipping over water, skimming with white wings.
Fragile as a dragonfly,
it lands, on tiptoe, on the cocklestrand.

A bustle of luggage and hugging.
News arriving: letters and papers.
Trucks scrawling tyremarks on the sand,
the cat hissing at a sheepdog.

The air hostess struggles with high heels
and the wind flapping at her kilt.
The pilot stops for a moment,
bends down, picks up a shell.

The forbidden language

In the slate-squeaking silence
of the island's only classroom
words spill out of a child's mouth
like milk from a tipped churn.

Too late to lap them up:
above her head the dominie looms
makes her stand at the front of the room
hangs round her throat the necklace

of a human skull
its eye sockets threaded
with rope that rubs weals
in soft neck flesh.

The weight of adult head
thuds on her chest all day.
She dares herself to wiggle
the loose brown teeth

to touch the grimy calcium
that's rough as lichened stone
not white like sea-washed bones
she finds along the shore.

The skull's an anchor dragging her
to the bottom of the sea
pulling her down as swell fills her mouth
and she spits out salt —

She plots that when she's woman
she'll dig up all the island's graves
and hang a hundred clanking skulls
about his gawky English-speaking neck

and hurling every curse her language knows
she'll drag him to the highest cliff
pitch him into the pincers of rocks
the gaping grin of the minch.

The last residents of Mistras

Byzantium became us, we who were the relics:
we liked to live peculiar among ruins,
had grown accustomed to the multitude of ghosts
that flitted in and out through ransacked walls,
the flakes of gold leaf carried on the breeze
and we knew that underneath the chapel whitewash
lay frescoes in the colours of anemones.

Stonework crumbled like goats' cheese,
wildflowers grew in the hollows of steps
or clutched at ancient terracotta
and we too clung like vineleaves
to the gaunt life of the mountaintop,
burning beeswax candles in the gloom of evening,
hanging heavy weavings against the nip of wind.

Our minds baulked at ancestry, at the vastness
of this city, home once to thirty thousand souls,
scampering out their lives at such an altitude.
Enough that we had found the bones and hair of humans,
frayed snippets of their cloth, their potsherds:
fragments that could link us to the splendour
of the time when our familiars lived.

We wrapped these tokens — skull bones,
broken plates and scraps of gold — in blankets
or buried them in sacks of meal, to be heaved
onto the backs of donkeys and clattered down the track.
We took them as remembrance of Mistras
when we were led down from these heights,
herded like animals into new pastures.

We lived too high above the world
and so they took us down
onto flat, accessible land, promised us amenities,
told us that only hermits would want to live up there.
We left our old Byzantium to the nuns
and they remain, bees at the hive of the convent,
devoted to their virgin and their weaving,

growing freesias and black-tongued tulips,
letting the wisteria get rampant.
They keep to musty rooms, hoarded with icons
and embroidery and photos of the year it snowed,
living off their threadwork and the few drachmas gifted
for their homemade candles, lit by pilgrims
who come to stumble round our old abandoned homes.

We, having our modern lives down here in the valley,
where the mist lies thick as blankets in the mornings,
look up beyond the spikes of cypresses
to the decaying rooftops, remnants of another life.
At night, between the shadows of the almond trees,
we see the tiny windows of the convent
glimmering like fireflies on the old mountainside.

Relics of the Pharaohs

Star-shapes sewn to leopard skin
the brown pelt crumbling away

Tattered shrouds of linen
their purples dusty and faded

Beads of amber and of turquoise
A crown of fine gold wire

Traces of ancient oil
in an alabaster lamp

Hieroglyphics in a faded ink
telling an undeciphered tale

Such are the tinctures of a dynasty
the trickles in the liquid of the past

Desert

Wind licks your face as gentle as breath
Sand laps like silk round your skin

A straggle of cacti   naked and spindly
A scatter of chalk-white rocks

Splinter-thin shadows of dune grass
marking the wind-wrinkled sand

You bury your hands   sinking them deep
fingering down past the heat

Fine sand sifts from your palm
Watch it fall as if from an hour-glass

and think of the soldiers who've slept here
of the hot bite of desert in war-time

Grit flung like spittle into the eyes
Bombs lurking under the curves of sand

Think of the young boys dead in El Adem
'tousled hair under the issue blanket'

of 'grey corpses on a dun sand
...full of the rubbish and fragments of battle'

of the 'six men dead on the sand
that was so comfortable easy and kindly'

Think of your father here in the fifties
setting up camp in a wind storm

playing at battlegames over the dunes
And think of the new desert war

a bandage of smoke wrapping the air
the stench of oilfields on fire

So many dead in the desert's bed
its sand stained with rust-coloured blood

Shudder as sun stoops down towards land
and the pale flesh of desert grows dark

and know how easily   how swiftly
this sand could mould itself around you

could wrap you in its dust-soft arms
and clasp and smother you

Leaving Egypt

Wake in the dark before the call to prayer
In the stifling night feel rooftop breeze
sip mint tea   listen for the cockerel

Walk along the strangely quiet streets
past sleeping people lolled in doorways

Buy warm bread for your journey
at the bakery   Hush the barking dog

Take the bus by the Nile as darkness lifts
and dawn like a gauze drapes over Cairo
makes all shapes hazy   sand-coloured

so the dull-silver dome of the Citadel
rises like a mirage in the half-light

and in the City of the Dead   ghost-life
shifts   among the mausoleum homes

Skirt the quarry where abandoned tractors
lie like insects on pale flanks of rock

Look back at those familiars   the pyramids
their squat triangles spiking the horizon

Take the long road out towards the delta
Leave the city as it wakens into daylight
Noises rising   blurry colours sharpened

as sun becomes metallic in the white-hot
sky   a disc of hammered silver

Buildings dwindle   fields begin
then desert   Sheets of sand laid out
under the press of the iron heat

Nothing now but a glare of parched land
till that thin strip of liquid   Suez

Cross oily water   rucked by tankers
Breathe the clogging heat   then sleep

and wake to barbed-wire scratching sand
a scar across the desert's skin
to show where Egypt ends

At Jordan river

In the graveyard beside Jordan river
the sultry air is musty with the scent of pines

Looking for the place where they say the poet lies
I tread soft needled earth   and here beneath the trees
among the Jewish dead   I find her stone

and then kneel down beside the river's edge
plunge plump hands   swollen with the heat
into sluggish greenish water
where others   fully clad   have been baptised
and there are postcards showing it

But on me no dove descends   no blessing comes
none but the lick of brackish liquid
on my itchy freckled skin
the hovering of a dragonfly
above the drowsy water

I'm drowning in a gush of memory
Should I collect some reliquary?
For Jordan's where they got their story
their notion of complete immersion

There was a church-hall cupboard
hung with garments such as Puritans once wore
We put them on   were dipped like sheep
and they rejoiced and were glad
for the crooks of their prayers
had pulled us in

We rose from tepid water   cleansed from sin
We dripped and shivered   were redeemed
We left wet footprints on the stippled floor

But once begin to have your vagrant poet-thoughts
and they will clamp you down and lay you out for in-
quisition on a rack of their own peculiar making

I fled   I swam in words
that came in waves   an ocean rush
an endless sea that could drown me in its force
or let me surf —

We are land creatures   caught between air and water
stilted between bird and fish   wing and gill
between the body and the spirit

Here at Jordan where a swoop of doves' wings
brushed the air   where river-water
laid a blessing once   the woods are holy still
though the water's stale with heat and drought
and Kinneret scarcely trickles over drying rocks

I go back to the pine trees and the poet's grave
I lie beside her on the bed of earth
and breath the musk of resin   Our words
are murmurs   the poems of the living and the dead

Between these whispers comes the sound of wingbeats
and above us in the branches there are doves

Suez

After a day's hot drive through desert,
this mirage: silhouettes of ships,
black shapes sailing past a crimson sky.

The vast canal, gouged out of sand,
is a huge tongue licking up the scraps of sunset.
Ripples are burnished, and carving through them
comes the ferry-boat, the lamps on its prow
staring like eyes, ploughing a path of light
through oil-sheened water. And listen,
there is music, the muezzin,
drifting over from the other shore
where white-robed men are waiting
as the dusk air fills with smells
of coffee and of roasting meat,
fills with the call to prayer, growing louder now
as the ferry-boat draws slowly nearer,
larger, becomes a ship of myths and stories,
a ship of light and prayer and music
gliding towards us on the dazzled water.

It touches land. We board, cross Suez
as the last of the hibiscus-coloured light
is swallowed up by desert dark.

I dream of the death of my sister

I dream the terrible dream
of your death by suicide, from loneliness.
Somehow I am witness to it,
there on the other side of the world,
watching as you're buried
somewhere in the middle of Australia.
A shallow grave. Fine reddish sand,
dust-soft, heaped over you,
covering the tatty clothes you wear,
your sun-bleached hair, your face.

Grief eats me. I can't speak of it.
Appalling secret, I hold it close
and silently go on eating and
shopping and making love and
telling no one though the knowledge
is so heavy and its image, stark:
your young body among old bones,
dead in the outback.

I am thinking, my life is changed now,
something so precious is lost.
But stumbling towards waking,
I'm remembering that, in real life,
you sent a letter from New Zealand,
the next place on your journey,
so how, the dream-brain asks,
can death have happened in Australia?
Clambering out of nightmare,
out of sleep's grief, I wake.

It's morning, the sun's shining,
and there's your letter
still on the table with the daffodils,
and your friends from Mull
who've stayed the night
are having breakfast, asking how you are —
because all of us who love you
know you're not dead, only travelling.

Daytime nudges the dream away.
A new image of you comes, standing up
and brushing off the ancient sand,
alive and grinning, resurrected.   11

Visiting the dentist in the 1990s

Two types of filling now:
one plastic, tooth-like, beautiful
one containing mercury, tasting of metal.

Fill out the forms: sign here
if you are poor. This is how
we choose your filling.

Tick your sexual orientation.
Whose tongue has touched yours?
Have drugs ever entered your blood?

The dentist is prying
in your mouth. The dentist is wearing
rubber, as a precaution.

A needle deadens pain.
Implements intrude in soft flesh.
Tears prickle. Blood comes.

'Rinse out your mouth' says a voice
handing you the cup
of tainted water, pinkish,

tasting of disinfectant.
Swill it round, spit out
grit, flecked saliva.

Feel nothing when you bite your lips.
The mouth of the dentist is speaking.
It is a white-toothed, shining mouth.

It has not known abscess or decay, nor
the lick of poverty. It smiles.
Says it's going private now. It lives

in a new country, as gleaming as its teeth.
Lives in a continent as white as its coat.
It's grinning like the Germans

who took the Polish Jew,
gave him a local,
cut out his tongue with shears.

Doctors sewed it back
but no surgery can restore
the sound and flavour of his words.

'Rinse out your mouth' says the voice
but the water is strange-coloured,
queer-tasting. Rinse, rinse,

take the anaesthetic, grow numb
to the pain. Ask no questions.
Keep your mouth closed.

Across the bridge

Skimming the bridge in a sprinter train
with windows fixed shut, I remember how you told it:
how, crossing the high miracle of the cantilever
you'd throw a farthing out and make a wish
as it fell into the far-down water of the Forth.

Up the bleak coastline where there's no fishing left,
out at the portacabin station, past the museum
where linoleum is history now, past the library
where you disinfected books for fear of TB on the pages.
And then the nursing home, where shapes of letters
spelling out 'Hotel' are visible in paler stone.

Inside it's pastel-coloured, smells of hospital.
I find you in a lounge, a wee body in an armchair,
your face puffed up with drugs, eyes glazed,
unrecognising, red at the rims.
A foam keeps gathering at your mouth.
You raise a shaky hand to wipe it off.

Your feet are wrapped in plastic pads.
How you used to zip about: Rhodesia, Cape Town,
Florence, Budapest, you with your bad hip and your stick.
But the quick bird-person that you used to be
is muffled up. Bundled and doped, she's gone already,
that perky self. The flesh will follow after.

I want to speed you on, I want to scatter
gold coins from the railway bridge
and watch them sink and wish you peace
and wish you death. You're on your way now,
swimming out to die, and all you need
is to be there, and have your hip not hurt
and have your bright bird-spirit back again.

I say goodbye, am out in this grim old town,
our family's town, where everything is transitory,
where the history I once thought important
doesn't seem to matter any more. The streets
are changing too, it's not the place you've known:
the folk are dead, their stories swallowed up.
There's rain, an east wind off the sea,
first sip of winter, and at my feet
the waves are moving in, icy and unstoppable.

In the Rothko Room

there is not enough language for the paintings
called by such thin names — 'grey and black'
'blue with brown' — that make you want instead
to curl your tongue round words like umber
indigo, viridian, in the same way that you reach
for images — of peonies bloated with rain
a sea-mist soaked in sunrise
or faded winter bracken by a loch —

       and falling now
over the edges you let the colours
fold about you like a shawl, like the melt
of lovemaking when the body fills
with violet or honey-gold

      and falling now
feel flesh awash as you gaze on these maroons
these blurry purples, luring you
until you slip into that drowsy place
where soft hues comb you to themselves
with gentle fingers, and show you
something of what made the painter
take a knife and slice below the elbows
as he gazed, perhaps, on ochre
cobalt, crimson lake

    and falling now
moved out beyond the skin of paint
that merely brushes surfaces of canvas
to try and touch the beating heart of pigment
the waves of colour as they broke so slowly over him.

Moving house

The hollow

When I was a child it seemed bereavement:
the old country, our Eden,
unreachable beyond those bulky hills
seen from an upstairs window.

Moving back across the border
feels like the same loss, same swoop
of loneliness: this hollow place
scooped out between my breasts.

The weeds

On a grass verge by the main road
there are mauve-flowered weeds.
I pick a handful for the green jug,
something living in the bedroom.

>   Horehound, willowherb,
>   dogweed, hellebore.
>   Dandelion, coltsfoot,
>   scabious, vetch.

Blotched face, scratched hands.
Packing cases, back ache, junk food.
Wrenched, I'm a weed creature:
straggly, unkempt, uprooted.

The china

In the flitting I have lost my
self. She is, perhaps, in a package
wrapped in layers of wadding,
buried in some box marked FRAGILE

where the frailest teacups nestle.
Oh hold me gently, don't unwrap me —
I am delicate as porcelain and
I would crack apart.

The light and the shadows

I dreamt of coming to the new house,
finding it filled with October sun
but it's muffled for days in cloud
that will not shift. When will I know

which way the light will lie, which
of the windows hold the morning sun,
and which the evening? Or where, at dusk,
the house will lay its shadow down?

The milk

I am recovering, a convalescent
from the self's displacement.
Each day, sipping a warm milk
flavoured with mending herbs,

I grow less weak. I walk
the new streets, edge towards
the light. And where I tottered,
balance is restored.

The lanes

Brick-cobbled, rust-coloured, cambered.
But bulldozed. Raw mud undersides
exposed. A new surface steam-rollered down:
flat black tarmac, covering bones.

The walls

The walls are dank here, cell-like.
Mould grows. I feel them, clammy,
closing in around me. But sometimes
they are pink brick, sunlit.

Sometimes there are exquisite mornings
when the walls are frosted and a pale fog rises,
soaked in light. And once,
among the gravestones on the hill,

17

I felt the west wind touch my face
as soft as mother-fingers
and saw the yellow leaves blow by
aloft in the breath of the wind.

The apples

My life slows to a rhythm of autumn.
I cook apples, bake bread. A yeast smell
rises through the rooms. I set jugfuls
of flowers on sills and mantelpieces,

in the sooty grates of old fireplaces —
michaelmas daisies, and gold,
rose, bronze chrysanthemums.
The house fills with their pungency.

The garden

One hydrangea: its flowers are greenish,
papery. Shrivelled rose-heads,
stumps of lilies. Weed clumps.
I dig the earth, plant out

the rosemary bush, my remembrance,
travelled with me to this place.
And then in stony ground I bury bulbs:
my yellow-petals, waiting for spring.

Interior

'It seems I am not myself except in my room'
— *Gwen John*

grey and white   light and shadow
how the air   softens as you enter
breath   comes easier

the slanting of the eaves
grainy markings   washes of paint
walls that hold you like fond hands

or draw away   and let you fill
the space   your arms stretched wide
skirts just brushing the floor
as you move from fireplace to window

a cloth   washed soft   draped
across the circle of the table
a white cup   rimmed with silver
will be sipped from   filled

brim-full of ambery tea
poured from the old umber teapot
its curves rubbed to faint gold
where the light touches

where the light is   fading
where the dusk comes in   like folds
of velvet   dove-grey   lavender

and the room   melts into evening
shadows   darkness   candlelight

The web

I am an odd and unknown creature here
walking the strange streets, invisible

as this city's clay-dust ghosts
that loiter in the disused kilns of potteries.

Home, I draw lace over window-glass, a veil
across a view of alleyways and weathered sheds.

Inside this worn brick house, I'm in a room
of wood floor, fireplace, painted hearth-tiles.

These things are the room's bones, root it
in this street. But the warm flesh,

the breath of it, comes from elsewhere.
On the white dresser there's a shell

washed up by the Pacific ocean,
on the mantelpiece, crystals of amber

sweet perfume from India. In the window,
a circle of silk, painted in Israel,

turquoise against the light. The careful
drawing of the café roof in Alexandria,

the plump blue jug from Alsace-Lorraine,
filled once with cool wine, a flagon.

Photos of my sisters, on the beach at Golden Bay,
in a winter field in Galloway.

The letters and the cards, from Ireland,
Inverness-shire, Sissinghurst... bringing me

the words of friends. And out of book-pages
come the voices of writers, no longer dead

or in some far-off country, but here
where they can speak to me, remind me

who I am. A web is made. These threads,
silk-delicate, yet strong as silver-wire,

spin from it, filaments reaching far
beyond this room. See how our lives

are linked, how close, in solitude,
we have become. This place is full of presences

of those who dwell among me, brush me
lightly with their blessings as they pass.

Unearthed

This is a town of ghosts,
lives on its china past —

museum pieces, Wedgwood's statue,
remnants of a time of fame and glory.

Inside its muddy belly,
in rubbish tips and building sites,

in cracks between the old brick cobblestones,
are swallowed scraps of history, an

archeology of beauty. Pottery shards.
My eyes have learnt to light on them.

I scan abandoned ground, seeking
my treasure, eager as a gold-digger.

These relics, mosaic findings,
the memory of what was glazed and fired:

curve of an old bowl, splinter of plate,
rim of cup. Potsherds,

their sharp edges softened by the weather.
I wash off earth, discover colour, overlaid,

perhaps, with a lace of hairline cracks
like the filigree of skeleton leaves.

And under old linoleum I have un-
covered hearth-tiles, rose-patterned.

How intricate the shadows of the leaves,
and of the petals, shaded pink or white

and scattered round with flower-heads:
tiny blue forget-me-nots.

Beside these tiles, I lay them
in a rough mosaic: rinsed smithereens

the broken, buried, lovely
fragments of a history.

The day the clocks changed

Wake to a morning jolted late. Something
is askew. The body knows it. Daylight is
awry. There should be blood coming.

Inside the body's workings, some gangrel
is at large, lumbering about
among the delicate mechanisms. It
devours. It goes out foraging.

In the lane a man is gutting a rabbit.
Offal drips into his dustbin.

Inside the woman, the hefty thing
prowls. She wants it gone. How
slow it is and cumbersome. Won't be
pushed.

There is a fur across her brain
growing like mould. Her thoughts
are muggy. They swelter. Also
there's a quick blade could slice
through all the bundled layers and
skewer you.

She paces round the afternoon.
The dusk's a long time coming.
The monster in the female skin
is restless in the queer late light.
Rattles at bars. Is
ravenous.

Cooks. Things
slither. Fingers
burn. Crockery
breaks. Darkness
comes at last.

She wakes to a trickle of blood
and the ticking of a clock,
a new day stumbling awkwardly
towards an arid summertime.

Motherland

I — The lace

The tattered lace of drapes
patterns with its shadows
the old grey carpet, my bare arms
as sun, late afternoon
slants through the nets

as I am always dappled
by the pattern of my mother:
semblances of gestures, words, desires
as she, the lacework of her life,
imprints my skin.

II — West country

I discover the languorous land of her birth,
a place where stone is the colour of honey,
where air after rainshowers smells of narcissi
and villages glisten with runnels and springs.

In this homely, milky country, sheltered from the wind,
I sense the presences of family, glimpse
the child my mother was, and see how much she lost
in being wrenched away, uprooted, taken east.

III — The dreams

There's a gentleness now in my dreams of her
as though a great storm had passed
and the thunder rumbled away

as though that filbert-nut of guilt,
its rooted, gritty irritants
had now dissolved as gallstones do.

And how tender the dreams have become —

> — I am helping her under a lintel

> — She is ill and I am caring for her

— I clamber barefoot over barnacled rock
and she opens the door of the house by the sea
welcomes me in and bathes my feet

I reach my hands down from the air
and hers rise up from water —

we meet upon the surface of the sea
that green elision
gleaming where we touch.

Revelations

I   The visions

I am a nun in England
inhabitant of Norwich

A room of stone
enfolds me
is my anchorage

I wake at dawn
when sky is pale as milk
and then sun rises

washes blue
as indigo will drench
a bale of cloth

But that May-time
morning as I sat
to face the slit
of window

there came a touch
a quiver as of feathers
or of ghost-breath
on my skin –

and visions came –

and then I was in
daybreak
clothed in light –

*

Noon-time
casts a light-shard
on my wall

A faint warmth
a honey colour
on my hand's palm

and yet how weakened
is this light
born in the crimson sun

and come to brush
my small pale flesh

So these revelations
are as glances
of a great light

dimmed within this cell
to what my eyes
can bear to look upon

II   The telling

'I am a simple creature, unlettered'

I have seen books
inlaid with gold-leaf
and traceries of green

words once spoken
set on parchment

as silver chalices
are laid out at a feast
each in its place

Can visions
– things as bright and frail
as candleflame, filling

for a moment, a whole cell
then blown to dark wick –
be written?

I dip
my pen
in ink

feel quill's tip
– swan's feather –
dusting my skin

I have sewn silk stitches
on new-woven linen

I have set foot
at first light
on a field of snowfall

Now I am learning
the curve of words, the
placing of them

on a sheet of vellum
that may last as long
as bones

'This is
a revelation
given in sixteen visions...'

This is
the gift of my telling

I am Julian
This is
her book

A prayer for my sister

Plumb in the heart of England,
a Sunday afternoon, and here in a room
with primrose yellow walls

is ginger tea, sipped
from the blue cup –
the tang, the good warmth of it.

It was you, fire-juggler,
ginger-lover, who taught me
how to make it, and I wonder

if you're drinking a mugful of the same,
over on the west of Ireland
this Sunday afternoon?

Later, cooking the first apples
of the autumn, tiny windfalls,
I listen to a soft voice

spilling from the radio –
an Irishman, here in my kitchen,
telling tales of a travelling circus

and you're there – you're clown self,
your puppet show – in my imagining,
so I find the picture of the circus-woman,

will post it to you with a pressed
rose petal from the garden where we sat
on the first hot day of summer.

I watch the flame-light of the candle
make shadows of the ragged shapes
of oyster-pink carnations

and am with you at this dusk-hour,
see you sitting there by candle-light
in a room you've made your own

with your lovely velvet colours,
your gathered sea-shells,
stones, bones, feathers.

This is the moment of prayer
as I cup you in my thoughts
and wish you blessing

and the light is deft between us,
the same lilting dusk
dimming the sky at our windows.

Can you see from where you are
the last shreds of the sun
dipping into the Atlantic?

Can you see a white moon rising
as pale as tissue paper
pasted onto blue?

This is how it seems, seen from
somewhere in mid-England
above the oak trees in the park,

the moon that pulls the tides
between us, swells the Irish sea,
and dwells in the nightfall

that lulls us, each of us asleep
in our hammocks of darkness,
and entering, sometimes, the stories

of one another's dreams –
as when you held the new-born child
all bundled up in purple

and then the thunder plummeted.
But you, in sheets of rain,
danced barefoot

and I woke to know your wildness,
your pleasure in the fizz of lightning,
the splash of rainfall on your skin.

II
Memorials

Memorials: Paris

Down, down, close to the grey water specked with rain, is a memorial to those deported in the war. Down below the ground, level with the river. Beyond the iron railings, the wake of pleasure boats makes small waves slap against the walls.

Inside the dim cool room, the tomb of an unknown deportee. A candle burns. A cell. Its walls are marked like honeycomb. How they crammed them in like bees.

Their destinations, the names of camps grown easily familiar, carved out of stone. The letters jagged, as though scratched, and touched with red that looks like blood. A litany of placenames. Fingers trace the letters on the walls.

History, running underground. Still as raw as shapes chipped out of rock. Still in living memory.

Those who were deported. And those who let them go. Those who did not speak. Evil seeps into us like damp. The river water slapping at the wall. The bells of the cathedral ringing out. A sung mass. A tale of resurrection. The trains are leaving daily for the camps.

(She told the story of the baby's grey silk nightdress, a garment made of hankies from a Red Cross parcel, stitched with thread found on a bombsite. A gift for the woman who was pregnant when they took her prisoner. They told her she could keep the child, and there was such excitement among the women –

The boy was born at dawn, delivered by a fellow prisoner. Then the camp commandant took the newborn son and drowned him like a kitten in a pail of water. And the mother, who had been the strongest, the bravest of all the women there, lost her spirit, lost all her strength, could no longer lift the weight of stone she had to carry on the building site, and only days before the liberation of the camp, she died.)

The place-names marked in blood. The river-water slapping at the walls.

Above ground, daylight. Trinket-sellers. The graceful, lacy stonework of the cathedral. Bells ring out. A mass is being sung.

Crowds cluster like pigeons, pecking for scraps – a prayer, a photograph, a confession. A video, a postcard. A candle lighted in the dark. The rows of white wax stalks set out like crosses in a field.

The trains are leaving daily – A mass is being sung – The river-water slaps against the walls.

Anne Frank's house

The whole house smells of herbs:
their musty grassy fragrance
filters out from rooms
where they hang in drying bunches

        tarragon / marjoram / dill

from dark rooms with windows painted black
to keep the sunlight out
to keep their bitter-sweet, their meadow taste

        oregano / rosemary / thyme

Outside, the streets are treacherous
and the city has grown vast:
no trams allowed, no bikes
He walks: the branded star
glares like a scar

At the house in Prisengracht
he goes among the drying herbs
touching their flaky leaves
the greens fading to grey

        parsley / chervil / sage

Soft handfuls, so light
falling through his fingers
He breathes in the scent   .
takes it like snuff

        fennel / valerian / mint

Above these rooms, the annex

        linoleum / wallpaper / lightbulb

He makes plans, carefully

        creep / whisper / tiptoe

Outside, the streets are giving way
beneath his feet

He bundles the family up here

        linoleum / wallpaper / lightbulb
        creep / whisper / tiptoe

Keep the slats across the window panes

This is where she begins
This is where she writes it down

     pen / ink / notebook

Her only secret place
among the jumble of family

This is where she tells
the story of her life
a story for the world:
'I will call it *The Annex*'

     linoleum / wallpaper / lightbulb

This is where she writes it down

     pen / ink / notebook
     creep / whisper / tiptoe

Dreams of fresh air / sunlight / dapple of canals
Dreams of bike rides / schoolfriends / flowers for sale
Dreams of death camps / bright stars / soldiers
Dreams of people herded up on tilted streets
of train doors / slamming

     linoleum / nazis / light
     bulb / marjoram / soldiers
     wallpaper / train door / rosemary
     dill
     linoleum
     diary
     diary
     diary

After the camps
after the end -
he comes back to the house on Prisengracht

     linoleum / wallpaper / lightbulb

     diary

The way his daughter told it

The Annex': her words, out in the air
out of their secret notebook
into the world

as easily as herbs blown in the wind
their soft greens scattering
as flaky as ashes

Memorials: Prague

The Jewish quarter on a Sunday morning of bitter cold.
Flakes of snow blow in the air. The cemetary is closed
for Passover. But through the gates there are glimpses
of graves: crowded, tumbled, aslant, the carved Hebrew
letters thick with lichen. Bare trees with clumps of
birds-nests, the rooks in the white sky calling and
calling.

Inside an empty synagogue, no longer used for
worship, a young woman crouches on the floor,
dipping a fine brush into ink. She is painting in tiny
letters on the wall: re-writing the names of the dead,
restoring a memorial whitewashed over by the
Soviets. The walls are being covered with the names of
the disappeared, the lists of them reaching from floor
to ceiling, tens of thousands of names, the whole
room will be full of them.

From a distance, the words seem no more than a
pattern on the walls, some kind of mosaic. They blur
into one another, something darkening the
whitewash. But go up close and you can see each hand-
lettered name: small black capitals, the initials done
in red, with the date of birth, the date of deportation.
The same dates repeated again and again: days when
the Nazis swooped down on the ghetto. And the same
names clustering into families: mother, father,
brother, daughter.

Those who vanished begin to inhabit this quarter
again: named and written down, their memory grows
visible in the pale wintry light of an unused
synagogue.

Across the city, there is another Jewish cemetery, vast
and silent. Ivy smothers the graves. Few of them are
tended. And in a huge empty space, to which the Jews
of Prague will not return, there is a carpeting of
violets.

III
The Gift of Light

The gift of light

All year the dream of coming here
to where sea reaches, sky is

ample, and all the shores
are close enough to walk to.

And there's a sense of something broken open
as gently as an eggshell delved with thumbs

of something offered, a gift
as plentiful as wildflowers

as if the melon-sun had burst
and spilt its seeds of light

that dip the water as the gannets
swoop, denting the shot-silk

Cornish sea she called
'half green, half violet'.

This gift, this light
that falls into the clifftop chapel

floods the glass-roofed gallery
and fills the house from windows

west and east, makes it a ship
whose sails are whitewashed walls

whose ballast is the places
where the late or early sun

lays down its slanting shapes
of gold, upon

a tablecloth, a bowl
of plums, a windowsill

beyond which are the swaying
cornfields, the hedgerows

where the berries are made garnet
in the glint of it.

Sun's seedlings shaken still
from the vast blue billowed sheet

of windblown sky, smelling
saltily of sea,

the sea that swallows in its waves
this day's end windfall –

bend of rainbow, the melding
of the water with the light.

In Hepworth's garden

A half-carved block of stone

Her chiselling tools laid down

Her clothes   these spattered overalls
hanging where she left them on the wall
of a workroom   gauzy with stonedust

Like casts they hold the ghost of her shape

Petals of white roses   a sea-green curve
of weathered bronze
                    Light   nesting like a bird
inside the mothering of a rounded form

A sundial of shadows   mapped out on stone
cast by threads   spun taut across
the air   between solidities

Scooped oval   a pool
of rainwater   rippled by breezes
into an echo of ocean

The rain   the seaweed's lick of salt
turning the bronze to verdigris

the fall of dusk at different hours
late summer nudging into autumn

the rub of weather
                    and the slant of light

All of this altering   as subtly as breath
as slowly as erosion   these forms   these
quarried slabs of earth's crust   these
hunks of wood or metal   made regal   airy
animate
            made into new landscape

by the sculptor who still moves about the garden
laying   as she goes   her unseen hands
the memory of their gnarled and knowing flesh
on shadowed stone   on grizzled bronze

Dreaming of it

'...that I had just left in Cornwall' (HD)

Presences surround me
ghost-frail   rock-strong

I dream I am among them still
and touched by kindnesses

*

I dream I am leaving
in a whirlpool of farewells

Her poems passed among us
sipped before we go

*

I dream of asphodels
those greenish lily-flowers

the word whispered over and over
like the sound of a breeze

*

I dream of blue   a wash of blue
I am lost in it   drowned in it

found in it   I enter
blue

*

I dream I am my seapainting
its colours are my breath

I dream I am a rockpool
entered and emptied by tides

I am the painter and the painting
and the rocks on which it lies

*

I dream the map of this landscape
marked with azure and gold

sea and sand   a thin
peninsula   seen from the air

I skim with my finger
clifftop and shorelines

tracing the lacy edges of land
the place where it nuzzles the ocean

and   leading inland   the cobwebs of lanes
the threads that wind through the heart

and tether me still in dreams like these
to the shimmering self that I left there

For W. S. Graham

Sydney, I took a pint of Tinner's Ale
as you took yours: down at the pub at sunset light
when the Zennor sea grows fiercely blue

round this windblown spit of knotted land
where you fled from the knuckled whack of the Clyde,
ran into the lap of the lazy Atlantic.

Was it here that language had you in its clasp,
tossed you like a slip of driftwood on an ocean,
caught you in its net like silvered mackerel?

Did it nip at your tongue on winter days
as you strode the icy edges of the cliffs
and cranked your frozen bones with whisky?

Did it enter your skin when spring came in
with the flecks of blossom, the cuckoo-spit,
the honeyed smell of bluebells in the woods?

Did it spin in your head in sun-plumped summer
when Zennor meadows grow drowsy with bees
and hedgeflowers spill tipsily into the lanes?

Did it hurtle about you in blackberry autumn
when bold winds blow in from the end of the land,
making you cower from the gale and growl of it

down by Madron where the rain in the trees
lulls you to sleep in the wide-eyed dawn
when sea is milky-green and dreams are fleet

and fat with words and you wake with a salt taste
on your tongue? Was this how it had you, Sydney,
all those years? And was the ale always this good,

this golden?

Solway

Love unfolded then, like crumpled petals
opening into sunlight,
unfurling at the stroke of spring

as we walked the seven miles of estuary,
reaching, after long mudflats, the beach,
the windless bay, the candle of the lighthouse,
waxen in the hazy air that hung like gauze
between us and the islands

and through an undertow of sea-mist
came the warmth of April sun
nuzzling at our dazzled, new-born skin

until, at dusk, the madder of the sky
shed splintered light on wrinkled waves
and sea breathed inland,
mingling damp salt air
with the scent of wild narcissi.

Fragments of this day remain: primroses,
pressed in a book, a sea-stained map,
and memories, clearer than photographs,
of glances, places, shades of light

and of your touch, when, swift as seabirds' wings,
you flew into the inlet of my arms.

(Above the estuary, the pale moon shifts, and the tide,
like a bale of cloth unfolded, is pulled towards the land,
a swathe of rippled silk, spilling over sand,
easing under the hulls of fishing boats and brushing
the tips of bulrushes, edging inland as far as it can
reach – until, gathered into narrowed, earthbound arms,
seawater blurs into river, a rush of it flowing from
Galloway hills, down into this saltmouth that it floods
with freshwater, licking at the briny tongue until the
dawn, when, drawn by the moon's odd magnet, the tide
slips back towards the shore).

After seven years of plenty
we're walking back along this shore-road
where the primroses are flowering again
and our hearts, new-milked each morning,
are still brim-full of love.

Out on the acres of the estuary's wet sand
the shelducks catch the springlight
on their wings, and south, past Silloth,
the hills make the pearl-grey outline
of another country.

Inland is a darkness of sorrel and wild garlic,
a deep green scattered by the stars
of wood anemones' white flowers,
and in a hedgerow, frail as eggshell,
are nested five new violets.

Such things become the sediment of memory,
the layers we gather over years,
flecked with the bright silt of omen

like this heron, fish swinging from its mouth,
flying up towards pale April sun
that rubs the muddy shallows of the Solway
into folds of silver.

Hermit

I

The convent clung too tightly
A nest of rules   A swarm of nuns
The breath squeezed out of me

I needed out   I needed this
The soft lush greens   the tormentil
the lapping of the water on the lough

the sky at dawn a clear-washed blue
and lapwings flying up from moorland
into myrtle-scented air

II

Silence   was what I craved
I have it now   such vastness
in the swooping fields

the hollow sky
How thin my whispering prayers
given to the wind

I remember the swell of our voices
at mass   the chapel filled
with waves of singing

But solitude   was what I wanted
I chose it   flung it round me
like a muffling cloak

And yet such longings come
for human touch
for a hand laid on my shoulder

for women's voices threading words
as easily as worn beads
shuffled on a rosary

III

I live in what was ruined
have crammed with moss
the dry stone walls

dug up scant land and planted seeds
I milk the cow   bake bread
and feed a suckling lamb

I am become almost animal
grubbing the earth for food
drinking the melted snow

have forgotten the look of myself
A smudged glimpse in the raintub
is all   a faint reminder of my face

Will my human heart wither away?
I speak with the souls of the dead
more often than I meet the living

I fast   My body shrivels
like a berry caught by frost
I have no need of its frail casing

Am I nothing but spirit now?
Sometimes flesh so lessens
it seems I am made of mountain air

and then the inner life
becomes enormous   fills me
I am swollen with its light

Or else I am a woman   whose bones
grow cold and damp   I am a mortal
needing nourishment of food and touch

Some days my peat-fire dwindles
Its small flames
will not flare

Some days faith fails me
and the huge place where the light should be
is empty

IV

In the harebell-blue of dusk
my window   lamp-lit
is a pale gold square

set amid the sloped folds
of the sheep fields   shadowed
by the solid mountain

Living this hermit-life
in my turnip-wrinkled skin
I make a lantern of myself

There is a candle-flame within
I cup with careful hands
against the wind

A fragile thing   I keep it lit
My own lode-star
to guide me home

Flowers for her

Since she has no gravestone,
no letters carved in marble
spelling out her name
where I could trace my fingers
in the grooves of words,

I walk this dusty east-wind town
searching for some other place
to lay down flowers for her.

Our footsteps fold into each other's
as I tread these old familiar streets
following the litany of names –
St Brycedale, St Clair, the Causeway
Asquith, Octavia, Ava

and here on Lady Helen Road
outside the house where she was born,
I feel the ghosts come softly,
brushing up against me
in the silences that fall
between the rumble of the trains.

I take the long road travelled by the hearse
but in the flattened, eerie garden
heavy with rose-bushes planted over ashes,
I cannot reach her –

for she flits, bird-like, over the walls
and out into the oak-wood

where, among saplings, I lay down at last
these unnamed, blue-starred flowers,
making a memorial as brief and fleeting
as her airy spirit set for flight

in a handful of petals left to wither
beneath a tree so tiny
I can clasp my fingers round its trunk.

Tracks

Beside the newness of this mourning
lies the shadow of another death –

that of my grandfather,
her elder brother.

A harsh old memory.
a gash I thought had healed –

but here is his ghost
still walking the streets with her.

Listen, and you will hear
both their voices

singing in the silences between the trains
outside the house where they were born.

Hand in hand, arm in arm
they are children, they are old folks,

they are spirits
flying from the harbour out to sea

to where their other siblings died
in Canada, in Pakistan.

They know, have always known,
the east-wind streets of this town,

they could walk it in darkness or snow,
she lame, he half-blind –

I stumble far behind them
trying to remember the stories

trying to touch the past they lived in,
to gather up the pieces that remain

all that's left of them
as their lives fade out of memory

grown blurry as their outlines
in old photographs, slipping

out of sight beneath the fuzz
of too much darkness, too much light.

Flour / the maid's tale

Flour: it sifts about this house
like falling snow: flurries of it

imprinted with his bootmarks
on stoneflagged floors.

I shake my cloak and a cloud
puffs out, a blur of flour

and from my hair a soft dust falls.
I am whitened beyond my years.

Miller, grinder, flourman. He
brings it home: it clings to him

like an old snowfall, unmelted. He
treads it into carpets, lets it drift

from coatsleeves, hat-brim. He
has a smell of malt about him:

stale, yeasty, sour.
I boil up water for his bath.

Afterwards, a doughy scum
sticks to enamel. I scour.

In the kitchen there are sackfuls
of the stuff. He gets the boy

to lug it in. Wheatflour, maltflour,
maizeflour, rye.

Cook's knuckles are worn red
with kneading. Too much bread

in this house. She gives loaves
to beggars at the door. They know

to come here, furtively. And she,
his wife, dainty, crisp as baked pie-crust

insists on cakes, pastries,
shortbread biscuits. A laden cakestand.

I, in a prim starched apron, bring
porcelain, come running when she rings for me.

Back in the pantry, Cook's arms are
deep in the flour bin. Sometimes

I dig my fingers in, let the soft stuff
fall through them like sand, and dream

of being buried in it, snuggled
in the great vats at the factory

where the air is thick with it
and the men's lungs clogged and silted.

Here there are only traces of it.
What gathers in this house is nothing

so they say. But I am endlessly
dusting, sweeping, blacking flecked grates,

washing smeary windows where flour
sticks to damp. And when I light the lamps

flour has gathered on the mantles,
burns up in a whiff of toasting.

Even my sleep is inhabited
by flour. I wake from dreams

of walking ghostlike through a haze of chaff,
of lifting up my arms and feeling

flour fall from them, drifting
in a heap about my feet.

And then I'm walking out
of this mottled, floury house

out into the clearness of the winter air,
into the light of seashore,

east wind. It's this, and the blowing washing
on the green, the cold fresh smell of sheets,

the call of gulls,
that gives me peace. Out here

the clouds are made of air, not flour,
and the whiteness of the snow

will melt away
with the warmth of human breath.

The silent order

She takes the vow of silence
She has no language now
in this new country of the convent

where tongues are nipped buds
that neither speak nor kiss

Flesh is cowled   dwells on its own

and spoken language falls away
is the shed skin of a chrysalis
the shroud left in the tomb
and she is lightened by its absence

The stilled mouth opened only
for the gift of wafer   His body
word made flesh   laid delicate
unspeaking   on the tongue

But sometimes in her head
the words are trapped birds
fluttering   crying out for flight

and her voice becomes a muffled bell
its muted clapper thudding

a tongue that longs to break
the vow   to crack apart the lips –

The air is spun with what's unspoken
– frail silks of prayers and rosaries
half-formed thoughts and untold stories –

a language never uttered
yet grown rich   expressive
in the quiet shift of hand or eye

as silence eases itself inside her
making clearings   as in dusty forests
places where the light can enter
and the spirit breathe.

Pictures from the life of Bonnard

A pink-walled house among the olive groves,
blue distances down to the sea.

Here on the hill above the town
he has opened the old house up to the sun

and in his paintings the rooms grow gorgeous:
thick with colour, vibrant with light.

                    *

Bowls of fruit on a crimson cloth:
peaches and cherries, fat blue plums,

ripe figs in their indigo skins,
a blush of light on each translucent grape.

The battered coffee-pot, the yellow butter,
white goats' cheese, orange peel.

                    *

She soaks in bath-water
scented with lavender.

He sees it stippled with ochre,
flecked with lilac, a lake at sunrise.

Her dappled, soapy skin
is full of all the colours of the dawn,

is rose, pearl, opal
and pale apricot. The bath

curves to her shape. Its cold enamel
takes on topaz, the floor tiles

are chequered with amethyst.
As she clambers out

into uncurtained light
her flesh is honeyed, washed with gold.

                    *

When she dies, he draws the shutters,
locks her room. The house has shrunk.

The bath is made of old enamel,
chipped and flaking, the floor

is black and white, its tiles are grimy.
Corners are threaded with cobwebs.

Fruit rots. Cheese grows mould.
Coffee tastes suddenly bitter.

He no longer plants the plumstones
in the orchard. Windfalls

shrivel in the grass. Birds
peck the flesh of ripe olives.

Paints are matted on his palette.
He will not soften them with turpentine.

*

Cowled in a blanket of grief,
he sits in candlelight, staring

at a painting of her. And she
becomes what he imagines

an angel to be, a creature
made of light and colour,

gone beyond the marks on canvas,
entering somewhere more precarious

and fragile, where she's no longer bound
by aching bones and wheezy lungs

but takes on wings, is lifted up,
could fly out from the surface of the painting –

Her room is locked and shuttered.
But here, outside the door,

he feels her presence, hovering,
as bees swarm round their hive.

*

The pink-washed walls have faded now
but down at the foot of the hill

there's still the hazy azure of the bay
and in among the deep greens of the cypresses

a glimpse of orange roof tiles
baked in sun. Unlock the old house

and you'll find a lingering smell of lavender
and linseed oil, a smudge

of cadmium yellow on a wall.
Open, creakily, the shutters,

let light filter in, a pale gauze
sheeted over dusty furniture,

laid in swathes throughout the rooms,
extinguishing the dark. Peer out

through smeared windowglass
and see, in the orchard, jonquils:

throngs of creamy white
risen up among the grass and fallen fruit.

A map of the light at Mochran

Into the muffled softness of forest,
down though a lacework of larch and spruce,
a slant of winterlight lances the darkness.

As the cold inner walls of burial tombs
were touched by a lozenge of solstice sun,
so an ancient calendar could be constructed

from notches on these wrist-thin tree trunks
showing where, at certain hours of afternoon,
their bark is clasped by ringmarks of light;

and even if these evergreens were felled
and the slope were filled with ghost-stumps,
pine-cones, nothing but the bones of woodland,

there would still be a needle of sunlight
tracking a path across the Ayrshire earth,
laying down a shifting map of light

as, on this farmhouse gable-end,
a beech tree spreads the shadows of its branches,
laying markings on the whitewashed wall

as always in the month past midwinter
in the last hour of daylight,
when out of the cluster of the forest

comes the moon,
rising over the rim of the hill
and up into the darkening, dusk-blue sky.

At Grange-over-sands

A spindly bridge splays over the bay,
the lace of its ironwork linking the places
once spliced by the vastness of sand.
Before the trains, the traders walked,
waiting all day for the tides,
for the oozing slowness of the estuary
to uncover the wavering path,
then setting out on mudflats
to tread like Israelites
the reaches of this Red Sea,
the marks of their feet and their horses' hooves
printed for a moment in the soft damp sand,
frail as the tracks of seabirds
that scatter the shallows at dawn.

But some did not return, were sunk
in quicksand: their buried bones still out there
where the oyster-catchers call,
their ghosts hovering over the bay
faint as the path that appears like a mirage
fleet as the seeping sea-water
that smothers the tufts of salty grass,
the speckled pebbles at the shoreline,
and then, as easily as breathing, eases westwards
out to where the sun has shifted
as swiftly, as imperceptibly,
as on this day in early spring
the blossom has opened on the trees
and the snow on the blue hills melted away.

Canaries

Out from the hot coast of Africa
a scattering of islands speckle the ocean,
the last of land before the New World looms.

This is where the slave ship docks:
a place of hummingbirds and bougainvillea,
of seacliffs and white lilies.

They call it paradise.
The crew are heady with it:
dry land, fresh fish, sweet wine,
rose-scented women at the harbour.

The cargo stay on board,
rammed in the hold. A mother
calls her daughter's name,
reaches out to touch her in the dark

but she's gone, she is chosen,
she is the one who is transacted
for the bright yellow birds
whose song entrances the captain
who will have what he desires.

She will not stoop in fields of sugarcane
but here, alone, is locked inside
a hot dark room. Outside,
the crash of waves on rock.

She's drenched in perfumes,
smeared with oils until she gleams.
She will become canary-bird.

Her smile is fixed. She cannot speak.
She knows no words. Her gritted
teeth, her fierce eye open
in the dark, her clotted
tongue forced into someone else's mouth.

Pale gold feathers float on water.

The tide smacks at the cliff.

The ship sets sail for the Americas.

Below the deck, his lemon-yellow birds
grow sickly, their tiny bodies quivering.
He brings them out to breathe sea air,
gives them drinks of fresh-water
and strokes their dappled feathers,
soft as peach-down.

Should he open up the cages, let them fly?
Would they hover by the boat as seabirds do
or disappear into horizon
though there is nothing there to feed on?

He has known slaves do the same:
has seen them leap from ships
and choose to drown themselves.

He plumps with seed, he prises beaks apart
to force in grain. These goods
are precious. He cannot let them starve.
Nor fly: he keeps the cages closed.

Her gleaming skin. Her fierce eye open
in the dark. She has nightmares
of her mother, stuffed into the ship's hold:

a woman gorged on gruel, believing
she is fattened up for eating
and weeping in the stinking dark
for a daughter left on an island
bartered for a songbird.

The squawk of fledglings.
The shunt of chains.

Feathers drifting up through rigging.

Eyes in the dark. Locked cages.

Birdsong. Saltwater. Sickness.

The shipload lurches out across Atlantic
dragging its freight towards another continent.

Sickness. Saltwater. Birdsong.

Woman reading a letter, 1662

Pale sun falls on the milky wall.
The table's draped with cloth
and there are velvet-covered chairs
but she stands as she reads,
her loam-coloured skirt
flowing down into darkness
and her smock, as blue as a Madonna's,
like a wide sky round the full-moon shape
of her almost-born child.

A crumpled map's pinned up,
showing the countries where he travels:
lands of fat coconuts and ginger root,
of turmeric heaped like powdered gold.
Each day her fingers trace the place-names,
weaving over rivers, climbing mountains
of another language. And his name too
has begun to sound odd on her tongue, which,
as she reads, moistens her lips, and her
heart beats faster, for the ink words
on the flimsy, cinnamon-scented paper
that trembles in her hands, tell her
that he will be home, that he is
on his way, his ship sets sail –

Her face is lit, as though for a moment
she were touched by a rich hot sun
that ripens spices, or felt the breath
of sea-winds plumping canvas sails.
She smiles, and feels the child inside her
wriggling to be born.

Airborne

The journey outwards, making for the island,
was a flight across a quilt of snow,
the oval shapes of frozen lochs
held up like mirrors to the sun

and the plane, our seabird,
soaring over the firth,
swooping past Hoy's jagged finger
staunch among the spume

then hovering for a moment,
holding us in morning light
that crowds the tiny windowpanes,
before we dip towards the land,
step out into the fresh salt air.

Flying homewards, heading for the mainland,
as the coastline at nightfall blurs with the sea,
I carry with me a gathered freight
of things invisible to cameras
but closely stowed.

There are pictures of new landscape –
a path of light across the sound at dusk
the reddish clifftops rimmed with snow
and a causeway, linking islands at low tide
glimpsed below the pale green waves –

and the memory of a curve of sculpture
echoed by the shape of waves
breaking on the harbour wall.

I bring with me too a fragrance –
the kindnesses of strangers
the touch of hands, the lilt of vowels

and certain images –
of an old man, a storyteller,
walking daily up the flagstoned street
to taste the sea-wind

and of a red-haired boy-child
who will enter into my dreams
hurtling down the sloping fields.

And there are other presences
I hold within my airborne self –

my sister, home after so long an absence,
whose thin, sick body I will hold tonight

and this fledgling, unborn one,
who, as the plane tilts into the wind,
I feel for the first time moving inside me
with a queer, soft fluttering, as of wings.

The stranger

Waking in the half-light of a summer night
when the sky is milky grey
and the garden faded to pastels
– pale roses, a creamy haze of elderflower –
I wander the quiet corridor
of this house where I'm a stranger

and passing by an open door,
I glimpse her in a mirror,
a figure in an old print nightgown
– belly as round as the full moon
that floated low above the barn –
and see her for a moment as ghost,
as someone from another time, someone
who is not myself

for as the old house holds within its walls
something of all those who've ever lived here,
so this stranger's flesh and bone enfold
another soul

the unknown lodger in my body
making ready for the daybreak
about to crack the darkness
and enter into light –

NOTES

Desert — The quotations are taken from Hamish Henderson's *Elegies for the Dead in Cyrenaica* and from Sorley Maclean's 'Death Valley' and 'An Autumn Day'.

The Gift of Light — The quotation is from the journal of Katherine Mansfield.

Woman reading a letter, 1662 — This is the title of a painting by Vermeer.